THE ANCIENT BLACK HEBREWS

THE ANCIENT BLACK HEBREWS

JACOB AND HIS FAMILY

GERT MULLER

Pomegranate Publishing

First Edition, 2019
Second Edition, 2023

FRONT COVER PICTURE: Aamu chief Abishai bringing tribute to Egypt, tomb of Khnumhotep, 1800 BC
By Macquarie University - Benihassan ProjectPhotograph of a 2-Dimentional object which is in the Public Domain,
hence   PD-Art   applies,   Public   Domain,
https://commons.wikimedia.org/w/index.php?curid=91632148
https://en.wikipedia.org/wiki/Hyksos#/media/File:Painting_of_foreign_delegatio
n_in_the_tomb_of_Khnumhotep_II_circa_
1900_BCE_(Detail_mentioning_%22Abisha_the_Hyksos%22_in_hieroglyphs).jpg

BACK COVER PICTURE: Aamu gazelle tamer, part of Abishai's delegation, 1800 BC
By Macquarie University - Benihassan ProjectPhotograph of a 2-Dimentional object which is in the Public Domain, hence PD-Art applies,
Public Domain, https://commons.wikimedia.org/w/index.php?curid=91632149
https://commons.wikimedia.org/wiki/File:Painting_of_foreign_delegation_in_the
_tomb_of_Khnumhotep_II_(circa_1900_BCE).jpg

CONTENTS

Message to our Readers

The books of Pomegranate Publishing were built from 5000 pages of the notes of Fari Supiya by his students Gert Muller, Anu M'Bantu, and Hermel Hermstein. Who is Fari Supiya? In the book When We Ruled, on page 1, this question is answered: "My colleague, Mr. Fari Supiya, brought an unparalleled rigour to African historiography that few researchers have ever equalled. I believe his contribution will set the very highest standards in African historical research for the future..." This is said about someone who does not have a university education, which shows the potential of Black people even without a college degree (we destroy negative stereotypes; **intelligence**). And while the association between Supiya and that author has since catastrophically imploded (unfortunately, a common phenomenon in our community; Griff and Zaza, Tariq and Umar, etc.), this cannot legitimately change the observation. With such standards as a foundation, it is not difficult to see why we were coveted by some on the Black side who wanted these books (to sell for their own profit) and some on the White side who wished the books would disappear (as if both were trying to uphold negative stereotypes; **theft** and **racism**). In a remarkable coincidence, both sides got their wish **at the same time**. Setting the "highest standards in African historical research" is clearly threatening to certain parties on both sides and comes at a cost. Nor were they finished. Supiya received a communication that a man in fake dress code was coming to his residence with the intention of inducing death by "natural causes" so as not to be investigated. He did not take this seriously until a man in the said fake dress code turned up wanting admission to the residence. Supiya reported the matter to the police and his concerns of the connection to other events. They gave him a case number and are watching for future developments. It seems like we were not supposed to make a comeback. But we are doing just that and are happy to be serving the community with a **transparent, objective, truthful**, yet unapologetic history after those who lack these qualities would stop at nothing to prevent us from doing so. Specialising in our history does not make us nationalistic or ethnocentric, which may surprise some. While such positions are understandable reactions to limited opportunities, they can cloud objectivity. If one is to reveal the hidden history of Black people, they must have objectivity as a guiding principle. By such standards we will fight negative stereotypes instead of upholding them.

CHAPTER 1

Introduction

In *The Ancient Black Hebrews: The Genetic Evidence,* we concluded that the ancestors of the first Semitic speakers entered SW Asia from Africa. There they found an aboriginal SW Asian population that originated in India. They resembled the darkest section of the modern Indian population. These two populations combined to become the ancient Semitic speakers of Southwest Asia.

In *The Ancient Black Hebrews: Abraham and His Family,* we revealed that in Genesis, Abraham and his relations were identified as "Aramaeans". This was because Genesis was written in the 7th or 6th century BC, when that name was current for that ethnic group. Had Genesis been written in the early 2nd millennium BC, they would have been called "Amorites". We also explained why Amorites were said to be descended from Ham and Aramaeans were said to be descended from Shem when one was descended from the other.

Abraham was an Amorite or Aramaean, as was his wife and close relation, Sarah. This automatically makes their son Isaac an Amorite or Aramaean. Self-depictions of Amorites are available from the Palace of King Zimri-Lim at Mari, dating back to 1700 BC. This is the time of Abraham. They show most of the Amorites to have had African complexions. But does this necessarily mean that Jacob and his family were automatically Black? Not necessarily because there were European types in the land of Canaan during the time of the Patriarchs. With each passing generation, their numbers grew. For this reason, we need to take a closer look at both Jacob's parents and the marital choices of his family. There is a great significance to this that **most Biblical commentators seem unaware of**. We shall examine this significance.

Recap of Semitic vs. Shemitic

Semitic peoples are those who speak Semitic languages as their mother tongue. Shemitic peoples, on the other hand, are those who are descended from the Biblical character Shem in Genesis. Shem, however, is a metaphor for the **Arabian tectonic plate,** as we discussed in *Abraham and His Family*. It is important to remember this distinction when we come to discuss **non-Semitic** peoples in the land of Canaan. The Canaanites were not **Shemitic** because they inhabited the African tectonic plate rather than the Arabian one, but they were **Semitic** because they spoke a Semitic language. One is **geographical,** while the other is **linguistic**.

CHAPTER 2

The Two Canaans

It is impossible to fully comprehend the story of Jacob and his family without understanding that there were two Canaans based on broad linguistic groupings. This phenomenon also partly overlapped with differences in **chief deities and how they originated**. What follows in this section is more detail being added to a subject that was first addressed in our earlier book, *The Black God and Goddess of the Bible*.

El worshippers and Ba'al worshippers
Every time we see the word "God" in the Old Testament, it is a translation of the Hebrew word *El*. Sometimes the form El Elyon appears which means "God Most High". The Canaanites in the OT worshipped *Baal*, the head of their pantheon. Baal's other name was *Haddad*. Originally, however, the head of the Canaanite pantheon was El. This implies that originally both the Canaanites and the Hebrew Patriarchs worshipped the same deity. Is there any additional evidence to support this? Yes, the episode of Melchizedek, the Canaanite High Priest of Salem,

who accepted a tithe from Abraham—why else would this happen unless they were worshipping the same deity? (See also *Canaan and Israel in Antiquity: A Textbook on History and Religion* by K. L. Knoll, Bloomsbury 2012, p. 325.)

The Amorite deities
The oldest communities in northern Syria were the NW Semitic speakers, like the Amorites. They and the Canaanites, as Semitic speakers, shared the same mix of Sub-Saharan and aboriginal Indian heritage. This is fully discussed in *The Genetic Evidence*.

In *The Family of Abraham*, we quoted Professor Daniel Bodi, explaining that the Amorites of the Euphrates had a deity called *Iahwe*. Bodi cites short inscriptions from the ancient city of Mari on the Euphrates, like "Iahwe-El", which translates as "Iahwe (is) El" and "Haddad-El", "Haddad (is) El". Haddad was an Amorite deity of the sky, rain, storms, and fertility. Based on this, we would conclude that Abraham, Isaac, and Jacob were Iawhe worshippers and considered Iahwe to be El (God). This is important to state because Exodus 6:3 seems like it is saying the Patriarchs did not know the name Yahweh. There are other verses in Genesis, like chapter 22, verse 14, where Abraham creates the theophoric place name *Yahweh yireh*, which would be impossible without being familiar with the name. Perhaps some consider it an anachronism. **Knowledge of the Amorite ethnicity of Abraham's family** and knowing that there is physical evidence that the Amorites knew the deity Iahwe settles this question once and for all.

Origins of the El and Baal Opposition

In 2000 BC, there were Hurrian kingdoms in eastern Anatolia. This region borders northern Syria. Further west in Anatolia, there were Hittite-related Indo-European-speaking peoples. The Amorite urban centres of northern Syria had minorities, first from the Hurrians and later from Hittite-related peoples. One of the chief deities in northern Syria was the storm god **Haddad**. The Hurrian and Hittite equivalents were the storm gods **Teshub** and **Tarhunt**, respectively (https://www.britannica.com/topic/Tarhun). They were the most powerful deities in their pantheons. This attracted Hurrians and Hittite-related peoples in northern Syria to the worship of Haddad.

Ugarit was an ancient city on the northern Syrian coast. In the Ugaritic myths, Haddad is a son of El, the original chief deity of the Amorites and Canaanites. Haddad, as a fertility god, was associated with an older fertility deity called Dagan, who dates back to 2500 BC. Newer gods often became the sons of older gods who had the same characteristics. This is how Haddad became a "son of Dagan". At the same time, Haddad was a son of El and Asherah, like the other Ugaritic gods. This is how Haddad came to have "two fathers".

In *The Ancient Black Hebrews: Abraham's Original People,* pages 15–19, we discussed the origins of the opposition between El and Baal in the Old Testament. The Amorites were made of two broad confederacies: the Ben-Simalites and the Ben-Yaminites. Most people can probably guess which one of these confederacies Abraham belonged to. The Amorites of Mari belonged to the Ben-Simalite confederacy, while those of Harran, Abraham's home city, were Ben-Yaminites. The Ben-Simalite confederacy had Addu and Dagan as their two most important deities, while the Ben-Yaminite confederacy had Sin-Amurru as their most important deity. Amurru was the Amorite equivalent of the God par excellence, rather like El of the Canaanites. So it becomes clear which deity is linked to El and which is linked to Baal-Haddad. This religious division developed further with the arrival of the northerners. The worshippers of Teshub and Tarhunt were northerners of non-Semitic origin. When they settled in Mari and its satellite towns, they were drawn to the worship of Addu and Dagan because Addu was Haddad and Dagan was his father. This is how the northerners entered the Two Canaans.

Other than religious differences between El and Hadad worshippers, there was another aspect that was to help set the stage for the Two Canaans. We shall see how this can be read into the Genesis narrative concerning the Patriarchs.

Hyksos and Euro Canaanites

From 2000 BC to 1600 BC, migrations took place from N Syria to N Iraq, S Iraq, Canaan, and the Egyptian Delta. These movements are illustrated in the story of the various journeys of the Patriarchs. They involved not just Amorites but also Hurrians and Hittite-related peoples who also lived in northern Syria. They moved to all these regions, establishing themselves as decreasing minorities from north to south. They became the Hyksos, who took over in Lower Egypt around 1700 BC.

Figure 1 The God El, the creator God in the Canaanite pantheon.
By Daderot - Own work, CC0,
https://commons.wikimedia.org/w/index.php?curid=41283672
https://en.wikipedia.org/wiki/El_(deity)#/media/File:El,_the_Canaanite_creator_deity,_Megiddo,_Stratum_VII,_Late_Bronze_II,_1400-1200_BC,_bronze_with_gold_leaf_-_Oriental_Institute_Museum,_University_of_Chicago_-_DSC07734.JPG

They brought with them the worship of Haddad. The northern element increased with each passing generation, and the worship of Haddad became the worship of Teshub under the name of Haddad. In Egypt, he was identified with the God Seth.

Figure 2 The Caananite God Baal or Hadad on a stele found at Ugarit. Baal is holding a mace in one hand and a thunderbolt in the other. He is about to smite an enemy after the manner of the pharaohs and even wears a similar kilt.
By Jastrow - Own work, Public Domain,
https://commons.wikimedia.org/w/index.php?curid=931147
https://en.wikipedia.org/wiki/Hadad#/media/File:Baal_thunderbolt_Louvre_AO15775.jpg

This situation meant that in the time of the Patriarchs, there were **two religious camps in Canaan**. There were those who worshipped Teshub or Haddad. They included Amorites, Hurrians, and Hittite-related groups. The second camp were the El-worshipping Canaanites, like Melchizedek. The logic of Genesis suggests that those Amorites who recognised Iahwe as El, like the Hebrew Patriarchs, would also have been part of this second camp. There were also **two linguistic-based camps in Canaan**. First, the Semitic-speaking Amorites, including the Patriarchs, and Canaanites. Second, the northern-originating Hurrians and Hittite-related groups. Their numbers increased dramatically in Syria, Canaan, and Lower Egypt after 1700 BC as a result of the Hittite kingdom's wars of expansion into Hurrian kingdoms. Some historians believe that it was the Hurrians who were the Hyksos. One Black Biblical commentator who made the case was Rudolph R Windsor in *From Babylon to Timbuktu*.

CHAPTER 3

Two Canaan Impact on Jacob's Story

Jacob: Black on Both Sides
We know Jacob's father was an Amorite or Aramaean on both sides, but what about his mother?

> Abraham became the father of Isaac, and Isaac was forty years old when he married **Rebekah,** daughter of **Bethuel the Aramean** from Paddan Aram and sister of Laban the Aramean.

Genesis 25:19–20

This means Jacob, the eponymous ancestor of the Israelites, was Amorite or Aramaean by both parents. This is another way of saying he was **Black on both sides**. We also notice that Rebekah's father has the name *Bethu-El*, or "House of El". This suggests two things. First, Abraham's kin were El worshippers. Second, Isaac went all the way to Paddan Aram to get a wife, as if he were specifically looking to avoid marrying a woman from the "other" religious camp.

The Deception of Isaac

The story we are about to analyse is learned by most people in childhood. Isaac is now in his old age, and the time has come for him to bless Esau. Rebekah suggests to Jacob that he wear a hairy garment, so Isaac will think he is Esau and bless him instead. The deception is successful, and Jacob receives the blessing. Few people who know the story understand why it happened, and yet the Genesis narrative provides a reason. The deception story essentially covers Genesis 27. In the last verses of chapter 26, we are told, and we quote:

> When Esau was forty years old, he married Judith, daughter of **Beeri the Hittite**, and also Basemath, daughter of **Elon the Hittite**. They were a source of grief to Isaac and Rebekah.

Genesis 26:34–35

This is usually taken as an anachronism because the presence of Hittites in Canaan is associated with the expansion of the Hittite empire into Syro-Palestine around 1300 BC. The migrations from North Syria indicated in "The Two Canaans" explain why ethnic groups similar to the Hittites were present in Syro-Palestine centuries before 1300 BC.

These verses are important for three reasons. One is that they tell us Hittite-related peoples were present in the Canaan of the Patriarchs, according to the Genesis narrative. Another is that marriage to them was disapproved of by Rebekah and Jacob. We can only conclude this was because they belonged to the "wrong half" of Canaan from the viewpoint of the Patriarchs. The last is that these marriages **instigated Rebekah to create the deception** that stopped Esau from receiving the blessing. Support for this last observation comes from the end of Genesis 27, when it seems Rebekah was **more aggrieved** by Esau's marriage to the Hittites. We quote:

> Then Rebekah said to Isaac, "I'm disgusted with living because of these **Hittite women**. If **Jacob** takes a wife from among the women of this land, from **Hittite women** like these, my life will not be worth living."

Genesis 27:46

We can now understand *her* motivations, whether one agrees with her or not, for preventing Esau from receiving the blessing. Yet so many misguided people have understood the attitude towards marrying "Canaanites" as a prohibition against White Hebrews marrying Black Hamites. How ironic.

With Rebekah desperately unhappy, Isaac asked Jacob to take a wife from the kin of his mother:

> Then Isaac sent Jacob on his way, and he went to Paddan Aram, to Laban son of **Bethuel the**

> **Aramean**, the brother of Rebekah, who was the
> mother of Jacob and Esau.

Genesis 28:5

Once there, Jacob meets his uncle Laban and his two daughters, Leah and Rachel. Leah has "weak eyes," while Rachel has "a lovely figure and was beautiful" (Genesis 29:16–19). These descriptions could have come straight out of a high school sitcom where the nerdy girl wearing glasses is juxtaposed with the almost physically perfect cheerleader. Jacob agrees to work for Rachel for seven years. On the wedding night, he enters the marital bed only to wake up next to Leah. He is then told to work another seven years for Rachel. Despite his anger at Laban, he works for another seven years and receives the wife of his original choice.

Meaning of Laban
Laban means "white" but also "shining" or even "gentle". Some commentators have tried to use this name to argue for the literal whiteness of complexion and that Jacob was instructed to marry from Laban's family for this reason. Other commentators have suggested that it refers to albinism. In *Eden,* we discussed how Igbo Nigerians with light skin are called *nwoko ocha*, "white man" (2013, p. 37). The *Jewish Encyclopedia* gives "glowing with wickedness" as one of its cited translations for the name Laban (http://www.jewishencyclopedia.com/articles/9568-laban). We think the secondary meanings of "shining"

or "gentle" are more likely to explain the name (https://biblehub.com/topical/l/laban.htm).

The Sons of Jacob

Jacob is nicer to Rachel than he is to Leah. According to the Genesis narrative, God disapproved of the favouritism and gave Leah increased fertility as compensation. Eventually, Jacob and his wives go back to Canaan. They are given two maidservants by Laban. All four females bore sons to Jacob. The result is recorded in Genesis 35:

> Jacob had twelve sons:
> The sons of Leah: **Reuben the firstborn** of Jacob, **Simeon, Levi,**
> **Judah, Issachar and Zebulun**.
> The sons of Rachel: **Joseph and Benjamin**.
> The sons of Rachel's servant Bilhah: **Dan and Naphtali**.
> The sons of Leah's servant Zilpah: **Gad and Asher**.

Genesis 35:23–26

These are the 12 tribes of Israel. We do not know the ethnic origin of Bilhah and Zilpah. The names are Semitic, but they may be given names rather than birth names. Servants, especially females, were often foreign. For all we know, they may have been White. What we can say for definite is that in the narrative, 8 of the 12—Reuben, Simeon, Levi, Judah, Issachar, Zebulun, Joseph, and Benjamin—were Amorite or

Aramaean on both sides. This brings into question the many modern depictions of Joseph showing him to be White.

Dinah's Trip to the Other Canaan

Leah also gave Jacob a daughter called Dinah. Genesis narrates the following story about her:

> Now Dinah, the daughter Leah had borne to Jacob, went out to visit the women of the land. When Shechem son of Hamor **the Hivite**, the ruler of that area, saw her, he took her and raped her. His heart was drawn to Dinah daughter of Jacob; he loved the young woman and spoke tenderly to her. And Shechem said to his father Hamor, "Get me this girl as my wife."

Genesis 34:1-4

Figure 3 A White Joseph weeping in Egypt, 19th century depiction.
By Owen Carter Jones -
http://www.gallery.oldbookart.com/main.php?g2_itemId=30588, Public Domain,
https://commons.wikimedia.org/w/index.php?curid=18474337
https://upload.wikimedia.org/wikipedia/commons/0/06/Joseph_weeps
.JPG

We are told a Hivite prince from the area Jacob settled in attacked Dinah. The presented facts may appear confusing. The words "rape" and "spoke tenderly towards her" do not blend well, but rapists have been known to present their victims with flowers after the event. There is also the possibility that "rape" here is used as a term to describe a male who sleeps with a female who he has not married. There are some societies that would not distinguish between the two actions. Or even a male outsider seducing a female of the ethnicity of the author. An analogy would be a Black man sleeping with a White woman in America in the 1920s. If it became known, most White men would have considered that "rape", regardless of the circumstances. It is not clear which of these was in play.

The sons of Jacob get revenge by pretending to agree to a marriage between Dinah and Shechem but asking them first to be circumcised. After the circumcision, when they were in pain, Jacob's sons put the Hivites to the sword. This appears to prefigure relations between Hebrews and Canaanites during the Exodus. At this point, we should ask, "What is a Hivite?" Both the Holman and Easton's Bible Dictionaries agree on the answer. We shall quote from one:

> Hittite and Hivite peoples of **Indo-European origin**, identified within the population of Canaan (as "sons" of Canaan) in the Table of Nations (Genesis 10:15; Genesis 10:15; 10:17),

seemingly infiltrated from their cultural and political centers **in the north and settled throughout Palestine**.

"Hittites and Hivites" by George L. Kelm, in Holman Bible Dictionary by editor Trent C. Butler, 1991
https://www.studylight.org/dictionaries/hbd/h/hittites-and-hivites.html

Figure 4 A more realistic depiction of Joseph imagined as an Amorite in traditional presentation.
Created with the help of DALL-E AI-Image generator

The Hivites are portrayed as reckless and dangerous. This antagonistic portrayal is reminiscent of how societies depict people socially located at the extreme end of "other". The repetitive reminders of how Hittite-related people are unsuitable for marriage can best be understood through the lens of the Two Canaans.

The Family of Judah

By contrast, when Jacob's son, Judah, takes a wife from the Canaanites, there is no specification to indicate northern origin. We also notice that unlike with Shechem and Dinah, where there was a northern origin specified, nobody stepped in to stop the marriage. At the time of the Patriarchs, the Semitic speakers were still in the majority, so on that basis, she was more likely to be an Amorite or El-worshipping Canaanite. We are told:

> At that time, Judah left his brothers and went down to stay with a man of Adullam named Hirah. There Judah met the **daughter of a Canaanite man named Shua**. He married her and made love to her; she became pregnant and gave birth to a son, who was named Er. She conceived again and gave birth to a son and named him Onan. She gave birth to yet another son and named him Shelah. It was at Kezib that she gave birth to him.

Genesis 38:1–5.

Judah married the unnamed Bat-Shua (daughter of Shua) and had three sons, of whom only Shelah survived. Despite no one challenging the union, the Genesis narrative **shows tacit hostility to the union by the way the children's conduct is described**. We can compare the different degrees of hostility towards these unions with 1920s America. If an Anglo man had tried to marry an Italian woman, there would have been family opposition, but nothing compared to the opposition that would have occurred if he had tried to marry a Black woman. One is simply a different ethnicity, while the other is a different ethnicity and race.

CHAPTER 4

The Joseph Saga

Origins of the Hatred

Joseph was the second-youngest son of Jacob. He was hated by his brothers. The reason for the hatred is given in the Genesis narrative as follows:

> Now Israel **loved Joseph more than any of his other sons because he had been born to him in his old age**; and he made an ornate robe for him. When his brothers saw that their father loved him more than any of them, they **hated him and could not speak a kind word to him**.

Genesis 37:3-4

While the above gives an explanation, it nonetheless misses something. When Jacob left Laban to return to Canaan with his family, he feared retribution from Esau for the blessing deception. He thought Esau might massacre his family. We quote from Genesis:

> Jacob looked up and there was Esau, coming with his four hundred men; so he divided the

children among Leah, Rachel and the two female servants. He put the **female servants and their children in front, Leah and her children next, and Rachel and Joseph in the rear. He himself went on ahead** and bowed down to the ground seven times as he approached his brother.
Genesis 33:33

Jacob's fearful actions reveal another reason for hatred towards Joseph. Notice how Jacob places the female servants and their children closest to the impending danger. Leah, the less valued wife, and her children were placed next. The favourite wife and her children were placed in the safest spot. Joseph was not just loved because he was "the child of his old age" but *also* because he was the child of his favourite wife. This situation created a setting whereby it would be Rachel's two children against the rest. This hatred was the direct result of Jacob's wife-favouritism.

Joseph's Dreams
At age 17, Joseph had two dreams. In the first dream, tools belonging to his brothers bow down to Joseph's tools. Despite the tense relationship, he told his brothers about this dream. **This action suggests Joseph was a cold and direct person**. Would you tell your brothers this dream if they "never spoke a kind word" to you? In the second dream, the sun, moon, and stars bow down to Joseph. This time, he told both his brothers and father. His brothers hated him all the

more for this, but even his usually doting father "rebuked him" (Genesis 37:10).

Jacob sends Joseph to his brothers, who are herding. When his brothers see him in the distance, they start to plot against him:

> "Here comes that dreamer!" they said to each other. "Come now, let's kill him and throw him into one of these cisterns and say that a ferocious animal devoured him. Then we'll see what comes of his dreams."
> When **Reuben** heard this, he **tried to rescue him** from their hands. "Let's not take his life," he said. "**Don't shed any blood**. Throw him into this cistern here in the wilderness, but don't lay a hand on him." **Reuben said this to rescue him from them and take him back to his father**.

Genesis 37:19–23

Reuben's maturity here is due to his being the oldest brother. He leaves on an errand, but once gone, his brothers are tempted to kill Joseph. **Judah** suggests they sell him to an Ishmaelite caravan that is approaching. Joseph is sold to the Ishmaelites for 20 shekels of silver, around $200 in today's money. They take him to Egypt and sell him to Potiphar, captain of the Pharaoh's guard.

The Chain of Events

Joseph became a servant in Potiphar's household. He was intelligent, diligent, and fortunate. He was given more and more responsibilities until he was the head of Potiphar's household. But neither a servant nor a foreigner should ever forget that **they act on borrowed power, and others can see this**.

Potiphar's wife repeatedly tries to coerce Joseph to sleep with her. When this fails, she accuses him of attempted rape, knowing that she, an Egyptian national, is more likely to be believed than a foreigner (Genesis 39). He is thrown in prison, which is interesting because Potiphar could have had him put to death. Why did he not? The **narrative subtly suggests that he was not entirely convinced by his wife's story**. In prison, Joseph's knack for interpreting dreams allows him to tell the pharaoh's cupbearer that he will be freed and the baker that he will be executed. The fact that **he told the baker his fate shows how cold and direct Joseph was**. Would *you* tell a fellow prisoner that he was going to be executed?

Years later, the cupbearer tells an unnamed pharaoh about Joseph when his royal dream goes uninterpreted. Joseph, now aged 30, interprets the dream and tells the pharaoh to find someone who can prepare the land for **seven years of plenty and seven years of famine**. The **not-so-subtle hint** is answered by Pharaoh making Joseph the Prime Minister (Genesis 40–41).

Joseph Encounters His Brothers

In the Genesis narrative, the famine of Joseph's prophecy affected Canaan as well as Egypt. Jacob sends his sons into Egypt to buy grain. There they encounter an understandably temperamental Joseph, whom they do not recognise (Genesis 42:29–30). The Hebrew history writer Rudolf R. Windsor observed that their failure to recognise him was due to the Hebrews and Egyptians both being Black.

We have more to add. In the West, we tend to think of people as being Black or White, but in places where there are many Black nations, ethnicity can also distinguish individuals. If a Somali went to Buganda, despite similar complexions, one would be able to tell him apart. But if Somali people had been settling in Buganda for generations, then it would be more likely to mistake the Somali for a native. In this context, the presence of Amorites and Canaanites in the Egyptian Delta would have meant they were part of the Egyptian population scenery. It would have meant an incoming Amorite would have resembled some people already present in the Delta.

Did Joseph serve the Hyksos?

It is not clear from the Genesis account whether or not the Hyksos were in power. The timing appears to support the obvious connection to the Hyksos, a time when Syro-Palestinians gained leadership of Egypt. It would have been easier for Joseph to rise in such an environment. On the other hand, it would appear that whoever was in charge had **staff that were unfamiliar with the Canaanite dialects**. At least, this is the impression we get from Genesis. After accusing them of being spies Joseph interrogates his brothers about their family, and they reveal the absence of two brothers. Joseph asks for proof, and they begin to discuss amongst themselves:

> ... Reuben replied: "Didn't I tell you not to sin against the boy? But you would not listen. Now we must account for his blood!"
> **They did not realize that Joseph understood them, since there was an interpreter between them**. And he turned away from them and wept. When he turned back and spoke to them, he took Simeon from them and had him bound before their eyes.

Genesis 42:22–24

Why does Joseph have Simeon bound? Because when young people behave criminally, the oldest person present carries the most responsibility. Reuben was absent when Joseph was sold, so the next oldest son, Simeon, bears the burden.

The family of Joseph
When Joseph became Prime Minister, every attempt was made to assimilate him into Egyptian society:

> Pharaoh gave Joseph the name Zaphenath-Paneah, and he gave him **Asenath daughter of Potiphera, priest of On, to be his wife**. And Joseph took charge of all the land of Egypt.

Genesis 41:45

It seems clear that those with responsibility in the Delta did not understand Canaanite dialects, hence the interpreters, and the incoming Asiatics did not expect them to. It raises questions about whether this happened during the Hyksos period. It may be that this was actually the late Middle Kingdom.

An etymology for Joseph's Egyptian name has yet to be found. It may be that the name has been garbled by time. Even the pharaoh's name has not been preserved, unlike the names of pharaohs from later in the OT. These pharaohs were closer to the 7th or 6th century BC, when traditions began to be written down. It is also interesting that the name of Asenath's father is almost identical to that of the captain of the pharaoh's guard (Potiphera vs. Potiphar). The Egyptian etymology of the name is "One whom Ra has given". Perhaps this name and its variants were common.

The significance of Joseph's Egyptian wife is that two of the tribes of Israel have a half-Egyptian patriarch:

> Before the years of famine arrived, **two sons were born to Joseph by Asenath daughter of Potiphera, priest of On**. Joseph named the firstborn **Manasseh**, saying, "God has made me forget all my hardship and all my father's household." And the second son he named **Ephraim**, saying, "God has made me fruitful in the land of my affliction."

Genesis 41:50–52

People who argue that there was a prohibition against Hebrews marrying "Hamites" should be directed to this and other passages. Notice how the Genesis narrative does not condemn or even show tacit disapproval of Joseph's actions. Compare this with the marriages and marriage proposals to Hittite-related peoples.

There is an alternative moral system running through **Genesis** that is never openly articulated but, once pointed out, stares one in the face. 1) **Despite tradition, being the oldest does not automatically get you the inheritance** (Isaac, Jacob, and Judah were not the oldest), and 2) **that which a man does will return to him** regardless of what justification is given for his actions. For instance, Isaac was deceived by Jacob when his sight was poor, so Jacob was deceived at night when his sight was poor. **The justifications provided in the Genesis narrative did not make a difference to the outcome.** Abraham, Isaac, and Jacob all married their cousins, and the result was transgenerational problems with conceiving children (Sarah, Rebekah, and Rachel). **The justifications provided in the Genesis narrative did not make a difference to the outcome.**

CHAPTER 5

Popular Images of Light Asiatics

The Red-Haired Statue of Joseph

Many people have seen the red-haired, light-skinned statue claimed to be that of Biblical Patriarch Joseph. It has fed the mainstream narrative that the ancient Hebrews resembled the people who play them in Hollywood productions. The statue itself is a reconstruction and there is nothing to directly tie it to Joseph or the Hebrews. Let us take a closer look at how the reconstruction was made.

Archaeologists from the Austrian Archaeological Institute in Avaris found a badly damaged head with no face. It also had an atypical hairstyle and hair type for an Egyptian. It resembled certain paintings of Syrians with light skin and a mushroom hairstyle known from the New Kingdom depictions of Asiatics. Light skin, almost yellowish, is suggested by the remnants of the statue's head (forehead and neck). Because it was life-size, it clearly belonged to an important person. Reconstructions have to be taken with caution but the complexion was based on remains of actual paint so it can be taken as reliable. The statue can be viewed at the following url: https://madainproject.com/avaris_statue#gallery-6. While we do not take seriously suggestions that this is the patriarch Joseph, we do think Asiatics of such characteristics existed. The reproduction from Lepsius, shown below, appears to confirm this.

We earlier stated that there were northern peoples residing in Syria, Canaan, and Lower Egypt in 1700 BC, around the time of Joseph. They had been present since the 12th dynasty and increased with time. The statue being touted as Joseph represents one of these northerners. The Hurrians and Hittite-related peoples formed their own communities in Syria and Canaan. They adopted the Semitic languages but tended to have Hurrian or Indo-European personal names. They also lived among the Semitic-originating communities as minorities and intermarried with them. This resulted in intermediate skin tones among Amorites and Canaanites.

The Hyksos
Before 1500 BC, the majority of Syro-Palestinians were Canaanites and Amorites. Although some had mixed with northerners to varying degrees, they did not consider themselves part of those northern ethnic groups.

They considered themselves Canaanites and Amorites because that is how they refer to themselves in their inscriptions. As long as children of mixed unions reside in a particular community, they are more likely to consider themselves members of that particular community. An example would be that if Ghanaian men travelled to Nigeria and took local wives, their children would be more likely to consider themselves Nigerians with a Ghanaian father than Ghanaians with a Nigerian mother. To get the latter outcome, those Ghanaian fathers would need to travel back to Ghana with their families and raise them there.

Figure 5 Light-skinned and red-haired Asiatics from Lepsius. This appears to confirm their existence.
By Scan by NYPL - https://digitalcollections.nypl.org/items/510d47d9-58fd-a3d9-e040-e00a18064a99 , Public Domain,
https://commons.wikimedia.org/w/index.php?curid=49838186
https://commons.wikimedia.org/wiki/Category:Asiatics_in_ancient_Egyptian_art#/media/File:Altes_Reich._Dynastie_XII._Benihassan_(Ban%C3%AE_.Hasan_Site)-_Grab_1_(NYPL_b14291191-38153).jpg

Figure 6 Four Foreign Chieftains. It is easy to spot that at least one is an Asiatic. He has the same mushroom hairstyle but with black hair and skin more brown than the pale examples. The Black chieftain with long hair is probably a Minoan.

By Norman de Garis Davies - This file was donated to Wikimedia Commons as part of a project by the Metropolitan Museum of Art. See the Image and Data Resources Open Access Policy, CC0, https://commons.wikimedia.org/w/index.php?curid=60939039 https://commons.wikimedia.org/wiki/Category:Asiatics_in_ancient_Egyptian_art#/media/File:Four_Foreign_Chieftains,_Tomb_of_Puyemre_MET_DT10871.jpg

Most Asiatics in Lower Egypt during the Hyksos period would have come from the Semitic rather than the northern background. Two fragments from Ezbet Helmi, the Hyksos palace in Avaris, show dark rather than pale skin. For some reason, they are never discussed as being Joseph or representatives of his people. It seems only Hollywood-type images get considered to be Joseph.

Figure 7 Another head with same hairstyle found in Avaris.
By Khruner - This file has been extracted from another file, CC BY-SA 3.0, https://commons.wikimedia.org/w/index.php?curid=91818853 https://en.wikipedia.org/wiki/Hyksos#/media/File:Asiatic_official_Munich_(retouched).jpg

Figure 8 Syrians with light skin, red hair and beard. The leading Syrian has the mushroom hairstyle, New Kingdom 1500-1400 B.C.
Nina M. Davies, CC0, via Wikimedia Commons
https://commons.wikimedia.org/wiki/File:Syrians_Bringing_Horses,_Tomb_of_Rekhmire_MET_DT226131.jpg

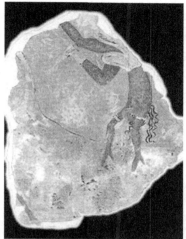

Figure 9 Fragment showing reddish brown figure from
Ezbet Helmi.
By AncientWorlds.net, Public Domain,
https://commons.wikimedia.org/w/index.php?curid=1415107
https://en.wikipedia.org/wiki/Minoan_frescoes_from_Tell_el-
Dab%27a#/media/File:Minoan_fresko_avaris_2.png

Figure 10 Minoan like fresco from the Tell el Dabaa Palace
at Avaris showing dark and light individuals. Minoans or
Hyksos?
By Martin Dürrschnabel - Own work by Martin Dürrschnabel,
de:Benutzer:Martin-D1,, CC BY-SA 2.5,
https://commons.wikimedia.org/w/index.php?curid=1436490
https://en.wikipedia.org/wiki/Minoan_frescoes_from_Tell_el-
Dab%27a#/media/File:Reconstructed_Minoan_Fresco_Avaris.jpg

One could dismiss the significance of these images by attributing the frescos to Minoan Cretan artists based in the palace and depicting scenes from their homeland. The strong similarity to Minoan style makes it likely they were made by Cretan artists stationed in the Delta. It is also possible that they were made by local artists familiar with Minoan style and depicting Lower Egyptians.

Figure 11 Joseph explaining the dream to pharaoh. Everyone is shown in rich brown skin tones.
By Adrien Guignet - http://freechristimages.org, Public Domain, https://commons.wikimedia.org/w/index.php?curid=8021318 https://en.wikipedia.org/wiki/Joseph_(Genesis)#/media/File:Adrien_Gu ignet_Joseph_et_Pharaon.jpg

A 19th century Exception

There is one painting, by Jean Adrien Guignet, that has a different quality than most from that era. Most paintings from the 19th century show both Joseph and the Egyptians as White. In a few instances the Egyptians are shown dark but Joseph is always White. In Guignet's painting not only are the Egyptians dark but so is Joseph. They are both depicted like Upper Egyptians.

Figure 12 Closer view of Guignet's painting. Joseph is to the immediate left of pharaoh (cropped).
By Adrien Guignet - http://freechristimages.org, Public Domain, https://commons.wikimedia.org/w/index.php?curid=8021318 https://en.wikipedia.org/wiki/Joseph_(Genesis)#/media/File:Adrien_Gu ignet_Joseph_et_Pharaon.jpg

We assume this is because Guignet had actually been to Egypt and had seen the varying complexions among the population. An additional inspiration may have been the Egyptian wall paintings. Perhaps he figured that those depictions showed the closest complexion to that of the ancient Egyptians. That may even have been his reason for including two such images in the painting.

CHAPTER 6

Reproductions vs Actual Paintings

Beni Hasan Tomb 3

If the dark images from Ezbet Elmi can be dismissed as being Cretan, one cannot be so dismissive of the images from Beni Hasan tomb 3. They date back to the Middle Kingdom reign of Senusret II (1897–1878 BC). The tomb belonged to Khnumhotep, governor of the Oryx Nome. In Row 3 of the North Wall, it depicts one of the most **reproduced and distorted** scenes of all time. The image is important because the leading theories are that it is of the Hyksos, the Amorites, or the Biblical Patriarchs. All three theories make them people of interest. This scene of light-skinned Asiatics paying tribute to Egyptians has been seen by most interested parties several times in textbooks and on the Web. The subjects of the painting are designated *Aamu* by the Egyptians. There is a good chance *Aamu* is derived from *Amurru*. *The Beni Hasan Visual Dictionary* has been prepared by Macquarie University in Australia with the involvement of the Egyptian

Ministry of Antiquities. Shannon Collis, writing for them, introduced Row 3 as follows:

> Two non-Egyptian men bring animals and offerings to the tomb owner. This detail occurs within the scene of an **Asiatic procession** on the chapel's…general view of the north wall. The two men represented as non-Egyptians have **skin painted yellow**, large hooked noses, and greyish-blue eyes. They wear brightly coloured and patterned clothing speckled in red, blue, and white. The men sport short, pointed beards with coiffed, **mushroom hairstyles**.
>
> Shannon Collis, "Leaders of an Asiatic procession, a detail from the tomb of Khnumhotep II at Beni Hassan," in *The Beni Hassan Visual Dictionary*: Khnumhotep II, edited by Alexandra Woods, Brian Ballsun-Stanton, and Nicolle Leary. Sydney: Macquarie University, 2018.
> https://benihassan.com/dictionary/Khnumhotep+II+Tomb+3/Leaders+of+an+Asiatic+procession/

At this point, we have to take issue with the Asiatics being described as "painted yellow". In the many images of the Lepsius reproduction that can be found all over the Web, they are indeed yellow. But this does not speak to the skin tones present in the original wall paintings.

The Metropolitan Museum of Art conducted a graphics expedition to Egypt, directed by Norman de Garis Davies, in the 1930s. His wife, Nina, made replicas of the images, which included Row 3. Below,

we present the "two non-Egyptian men" in de Garis Davies' replica, and we can in no way describe them as "yellow".
https://www.metmuseum.org/art/collection/search/544548).

Figure 13 Reproduction of Amorites/Canaanites bringing tribute to Egyptians. They Asiatics are shown yellow, but it is not an original. Pay special attention to the two yellow men heading the Asiatic delegation.
By NebMaatRa - This file has been extracted from another file, CC BY-SA 3.0, https://commons.wikimedia.org/w/index.php?curid=91638481
https://en.wikipedia.org/wiki/Hyksos#/media/File:Drawing_of_the_proc
ession_of_the_Aamu_group_tomb_of_Khnumhotep_II_at_Beni_Hassan.jpg

In *The Ancient Black Hebrews: Unmistakable Proof in Colour,* we explained that different versions of the same image might have different complexions because of lighting. It raises the question of whether De Garis Davies' replica was accurate. We can answer that question by presenting the actual tomb paintings below of both "non-Egyptian men". If anything, the leader of the Asiatic procession is slightly darker than in the De Garis Davies replica. Neither man can be described as "yellow". In fairness to De Garies Davis, her given complexions are largely accurate. Especially in comparison to Lepsius.

This discrepancy between the image as it appears in textbooks and the actual tomb painting should be a wakeup call when it comes to blindly trusting images without verifying whether they are originals.

Figure 14 Replica of Nina de Garis Davies shows the Asiatics were far darker than shown by Lepsius, but this also is not an original.
OA Public Domain,
https://creativecommons.org/publicdomain/zero/1.0/
https://www.metmuseum.org/art/collection/search/544548

The other Asiatic men and women in the procession are lighter than the two leading men, but they are not "yellow" either. They are the kind of brown associated with people of African descent who have some European ancestry. There are comparable depictions of Amorites, from Mari on the Euphrates, with intermediate complexions, shown in *Abraham and his*

Family. The best interpretation of the ethnic identity of the Asiatics is that they are Amorites. This is the same broad ethnicity as the Patriarchs.

Figure 15 Abisha, Amorite chief with Egyptian complexion. Stone surface shows it is not a replica even if we did not know the source. The lightness of the background lets us know it is not a darkened image.
By Macquarie University - Benihassan ProjectPhotograph of a 2-Dimentional object which is in the Public Domain, hence PD-Art applies, Public Domain,
https://commons.wikimedia.org/w/index.php?curid=91632148
https://en.wikipedia.org/wiki/Hyksos#/media/File:Painting_of_foreign_delegation_in_the_tomb_of_Khnumhotep_II_circa_1900_BCE_(Detail_mentioning_%22Abisha_the_Hyksos%22_in_hieroglyphs).jpg

Who are the Asiatics?

Where does the idea that these images represent Hyksos come from? It comes from the tomb inscription. In the published Archaeological Survey of the Beni Hasan Exploration, the inscription accompanying the image is given as:

> The year VI…Usersen II, the number of Aamu brought by the son of the ha-prince, Chnemhotep…Aamu of Shu, number amounting to 37.

Beni Hasan Part I by Percy Newberry; Kegan Paul, Trench, Trubner & Co., 1893, p. 69.

Figure 16 An Amorite believed to be a gazelle tamer.
By Macquarie University - Benihassan ProjectPhotograph of a 2-Dimentional object which is in the Public Domain, hence PD-Art applies, Public Domain,
https://commons.wikimedia.org/w/index.php?curid=91632149
https://commons.wikimedia.org/wiki/File:Painting_of_foreign_delegation_in_the_tomb_of_Khnumhotep_II_(circa_1900_BCE).jpg

Figure 17 The lighter Aamu behind the two darker ones in the Khnumhotep II tomb.
By Kurohito - Own work, CC BY-SA 3.0,
https://commons.wikimedia.org/w/index.php?curid=4405330
https://commons.wikimedia.org/wiki/File:Procession_of_the_Aamu,_To
mb_of_Khnumhotep_II_(composite_version).jpg#/media/File:Beni-
Hassan-Asiatiques1.jpg

The leader is given the caption "hak-prince of the desert, Abesha". Collis has comments that shed light on both the title and personal name:

> He is given the caption **ḥkȝ ḫȝst** (**'ruler** of a foreign land, Ibsha'), presenting **the first recorded** Middle Kingdom usage of the title. Scholars agree on a **northwest Semitic origin for Jbšȝ's name**. It has been equated with Abi-shai ('my father is king') and Abi-sharie ('my father is strong').

Collis (2018)
https://benihassan.com/dictionary/Khnumhotep+II+Tomb+3/Le
aders+of+an+Asiatic+procession/

The phrase *kha khasut,* "ruler of a foreign land," is where the term "Hyksos" is derived from. The name Abisha occurs in the Bible (1 Chron. 11–21) as one of the three mightiest warriors of King David. The Biblical connection of the name is one of the reasons why they are seen as related to the Hebrew Patriarchs. These kinds of names would have occurred among Amorites. Interestingly, **all** of these Asiatics have black hair. Red hair and pale skin occurred among the Canaanites of European type.

Figure 18 Even the light brown Amorites look Black. Does their hair look different from Egyptian hair? (cropped).
By Kurohito - Own work, CC BY-SA 3.0,
https://commons.wikimedia.org/w/index.php?curid=4405330
https://commons.wikimedia.org/wiki/File:Procession_of_the_Aamu,_To
mb_of_Khnumhotep_II_(composite_version).jpg#/media/File:Beni-
Hassan-Asiatiques1.jpg

Hamites vs. Hebrews

We have highlighted how mainstreamers have often presented a lighter version of this image. The original complexions, however, can still cause misrepresentation, even if unintentional. Sometimes an image ends where it ends, but if more were shown, it would give a different impression.

Figure 19 Amorite or Aamu women shown with white headbands (cropped).
By Kurohito - Own work, CC BY-SA 3.0,
https://commons.wikimedia.org/w/index.php?curid=4405330
https://commons.wikimedia.org/wiki/File:Procession_of_the_Aamu,_To
mb_of_Khnumhotep_II_(composite_version).jpg#/media/File:Beni-
Hassan-Asiatiques1.jpg

If one shows only the brown Asiatics in the same frame as the darker brown Egyptians, **it accentuates the complexion difference between the Egyptians and**

the Asiatics. If the darker brown Asiatics were included in the image, it would show that the Asiatic range of complexions included the darker brown of the Egyptians. Such images often become popular not only in the mainstream but also among those in the Black community who promote the idea that the **ancient Hebrews were not Black**.

Figure 20 A comparison of Amorites and Egyptians minus the darker Amorites. Their absence creates a greater contrast between the two.
By Kurohito - Own work, CC BY-SA 3.0,
https://commons.wikimedia.org/w/index.php?curid=4405330
https://commons.wikimedia.org/wiki/File:Procession_of_the_Aamu,_To mb_of_Khnumhotep_II_(composite_version).jpg#/media/File:Beni-Hassan-Asiatiques1.jpg

Even some of those who promote the idea that the **ancient Hebrews were Black** have gone along with this misunderstanding. This has led them to devise crass equations to maintain their position. They show a dark Black person with the caption "Hamite" and a lighter Black person with the caption "Hebrew".

This is done as if they do not understand that the only difference between the two is varying amounts of European ancestry. One web user clowned this kind of presentation by showing a darker and lighter picture of Michael Jackson with the captions "Hamite", for the darker one, and "Hebrew" for the lighter one. Silliness in the Black history community needs to be called out.

Figure 21 Abisha and an Egyptian official of the same complexion.
By Macquarie University - Benihassan ProjectPhotograph of a 2-Dimentional object which is in the Public Domain, hence PD-Art applies, Public Domain,
https://commons.wikimedia.org/w/index.php?curid=91632148

For Joseph to be mistaken for an Egyptian, it is likely that he was an Amorite of Abisha's complexion. **This image is the closest we currently have, from Egypt, to the appearance of Jacob and his family**. The moral of the story is that if you **know the tricks and ask the right questions,** you will not need to employ crass arguments to support your case.

Conclusion

One cannot understand the story of the Patriarchs, in Genesis if they do not understand the Two Canaans. Jacob came from an Amorite/Aramaean Black lineage on both sides. His mother insisted that he marry someone of the same lineage. When the Patriarchs veered from this tradition, and we find no overt disapproval reported, it was in instances where the spouses were of Semitic or Egyptian ethno-linguistic origin. Judah and Joseph, the two most well-known of Jacob's children, married an indigenous Canaanite and an Egyptian, respectively. When they veer from this tradition and we find staunch disapproval, it is in instances where the intended spouses are of northern ethno-linguistic origin. **No other Biblical commentator has ever brought attention to this phenomenon**.

At the root of the disapproval appears to be the religious difference between El worshippers and those who would later be known as Baal worshippers. The irony is that, historically, Biblical commentators have portrayed Hebrew Patriarch marriage choices as an avoidance of marrying Hamites, with all the racial implications of that view point. We are happy to play our role in correcting the misconception.

Conclusion

Black history deserves to be more than just a presentation of seemingly Black individuals. Forms of evidence have to be explained and subjected to first class reasoning. Seemingly contrary evidence also needs to be presented and discussed. This does not always happen. Our history should be presented to us in a way that shows the complexity of the issue, even if in simplified form. When we understand complexity it influences how we view everything else. We become less easy to manipulate and are better able to spot deception, both in history and in life (and from both White *and* Black). Pomegranate Publishing is Black history leaving no stone unturned. We believe it is the history Black people deserve. A history that can withstand mainstream scrutiny. That is why negative circumstances were created for us which resulted in us disappearing for over a year. We are back better and stronger but the battle is not over. We ask you to leave honest reviews of this work because those who created negative circumstances for us will certainly sponsor dishonest ones. Thank you in advance for your support. We shall leave you with a statement about what we stand for.

We Believe
We are Pomegranate Publishing and we believe the following:
We believe **Black people deserve the same quality of history as everyone else**. We believe that in a book

Black readers deserve the details to verify what they have read. We believe that in a book Black readers deserve the details to verify whether the writer is a "Doctor" if so claimed. We believe that there should be standards as to what is expected and accepted in Black history. We believe that transparency is the best promoter of honest behaviour both in history and in life. We believe that whatever your practices in writing history will be your practices in living life. We believe that the power of the collective is incredible. We believe that two can achieve more than one, and four can achieve more than two. We believe that the collective is made up of individuals, and we forget this at our peril. We believe that if you suppress the individual under the pretext of supporting the collective, eventually you will end up with no collective at all. We believe that ideology is a good servant but a bad master, whether for Black people or anyone else. We believe that **when ideology serves people, there is a great chance for happiness and reason, but when people serve ideology, there is a great chance for misery and tyranny**. We believe refusing to address the negative will not stop us from encountering it. We believe that everyone should know what they bring to the household table and the community table and should be able to openly state so. We believe that if you ask someone what they bring to the table, you cannot accuse them of boastfulness when they answer. We believe that agreement on everything should not be expected from community colleagues when you cannot get it from your own family. We believe that Black people should be treating each other better than we currently are. We believe that community improvement should not be used as a pretext for taking away the choices of others. We believe that a community that does not respect choice will not respect consent either, so consider carefully what choice-disapproving attitudes you foster and encourage. We believe that double standards and hypocrisy are ugly coming from anyone. We believe that we should start questioning the things we agree with **as much as we question the things we disagree with**. We believe that there would be no reason for stating all of this if it were already being practiced in our community.

Also, From The Pomegranate Library

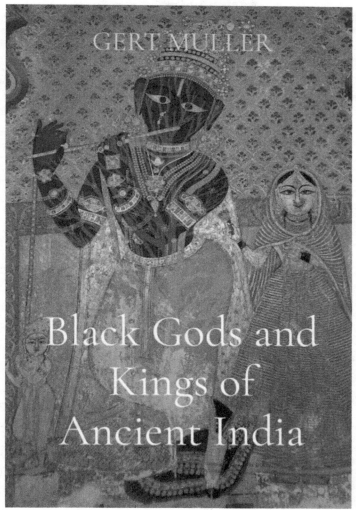

https://www.amazon.com/gp/product/B0CNCXRMBS?

https://www.amazon.com/gp/product/B0CQVQLCDR?

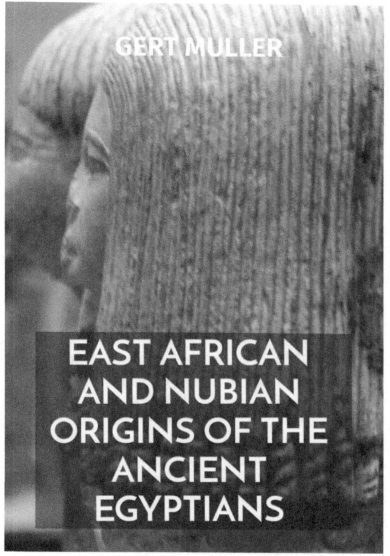

https://www.amazon.com/gp/product/B0CNCYQWQ4?

https://www.amazon.com/gp/product/B0CS9TW933?

GERT MULLER

THE ANCIENT
BLACK
HEBREWS
ABRAHAM'S ORIGINAL PEOPLE

https://www.amazon.com/gp/product/B0CNLCCDDD?

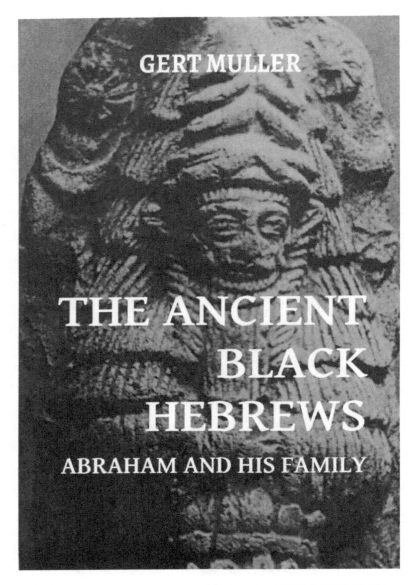

https://www.amazon.com/gp/product/B0CNHFJDVY?

https://www.amazon.com/gp/product/B0CNCW931L?

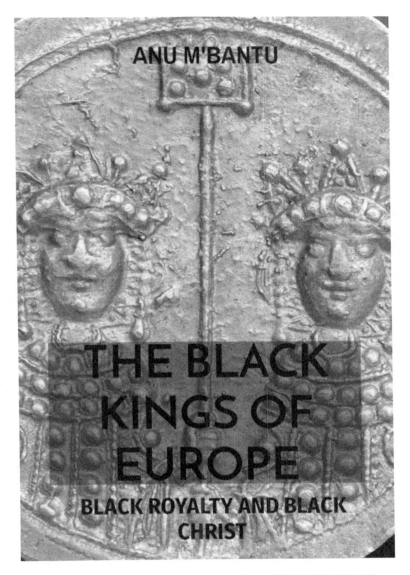

UNMISTAKABLY
BLACK
SCULPTURE AND PAINTINGS
FROM THE WORLD'S FIRST
CIVILIZATIONS

ANU M'BANTU

https://www.amazon.com/dp/B0D4LSN7K8

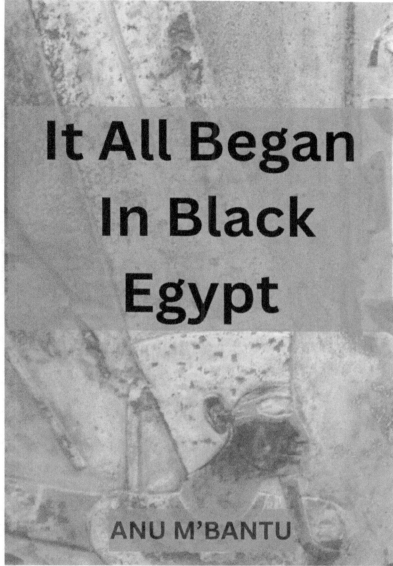

It All Began In Black Egypt

ANU M'BANTU

https://www.amazon.com/gp/product/B0D57GMFD1

ANU M'BANTU

The Black IQ Question Answered

https://www.amazon.com/Black-Question-Answered-History-Stands/dp/B0D6Y2B288/

About The Author

Gert Muller has been a free lance journalist's investigator for over 30 years in Southern Africa and Britain. He has been researching the history of Black people in Asia and the Bible for just as long. Articles he has researched have ap peared in such publications as The People's Voice Newspaper, based in Harare, and West Africa Magazine, based in London. Gert Muller only publishes his books through Pomegranate Publishing.

Made in the USA
Columbia, SC
24 October 2024

45012952R00043